Cold Weather Dreams

Written by
Jessie Michelle

COLD WEATHER DREAMS

Written & arranged by Jessie Michelle

Cover photo by Ikon Republik

All rights reserved. No part of this publication may be reproduced, distributed, or transmitted in any form or by any means, including photocopying, recording, or other electronic or mechanical methods, without the prior written permission of the publisher, except in brief quotations embodied in critical reviews, citations, and literary journals for noncommercial uses permitted by copyright law.

To every tear that has left my body.
You fought to find some sort of lesson in all the pain.
Through sleepless nights and bags of tissues.
This is for you. This is for me.

COLD WEATHER DREAMS

This cold weather dream.
Drunken memories and forgotten promises.
You reach for me like I never left your side
and I stay as though I have nowhere else to go.
And despite all the options,
to our left and right,
we touch lips and kiss everything else goodbye.

And then, I wake.

NUMB

Give me midnight and the sadness
that falls between empty sheets.
Wrinkled linens and sweat-stained pillowcases
no longer adorn my bed.
I am left with an unmoved pillow
and the memory of you.
You are gone and now, I find myself numb.
I want to feel everything that I am missing.
I want to hear your voice calling out to me.
But, I am here alone and finally realizing
that empty bed you left me with,
is hard to silence and at this point,
I'm not even sure that I want to.

BRIDGES

We crossed bridges we never knew we had built.
Held onto to railings,
when we used to hold on to each other.
With every breath that we took,
we lost a little bit of ourselves.
Of who we were when we were together.

We are crossing lines without dotting "i's".
Forgetting that everything we were, was meant to be.
Like an echo in the wind, we are slowly fading away.
I feel myself pulling and pulling to try and keep
a hold of everything we have brought with us.

But I am losing my grip,
and soon, I know I will lose you.

MORNING COFFEE

    The sun was bright this morning. We sat as it peaked in through the curtains and bounced off the speckles of dust that was floating mid-air. We chased after the light as if we were trying to collect it and bottle it up. It brought a warmth that was familiar but also shined a light on the quietness that we were sitting in. There is a silence that stays as if it was invited. Things had changed. Ours isn't (anymore) the kind of love that sat and stared. We hadn't stared in so long.

    Your eyes drifted to avoid mine; with or without intention, I wasn't quite sure. But they no longer met mine with a passion that was screaming to be put out. You didn't reach across the table. Tracing my knuckles with your calloused hands, slowly moving your way up my arm and landing on the back of my neck. They used to live there. You would spell out the same three words only to have me guess them over and over.

  "I love you".

  I would smile, pretend to be clueless, and ask you to do it one more time. I always knew what you were saying but would do anything and everything I could to keep you touching me just a little longer.

  I sat quietly and watched your hands as they grabbed the coffee cup. They are strong. Mine are but a fading shadow compared to yours. I always loved your hands. The way your knuckles would rise and fall as they would squeeze my thigh. Like a heartbeat, I could see. Without looking, your fingers would find their way between the handle and the mug and I suddenly missed the way they used to find me. So gently, but with so much purpose. Blindly, but seeing all of me.

You used to know every inch of my body. Every curve, every detour.

You knew which way to travel and which roads to avoid. But now, you needed a map to even get started. I was foreign territory. A world undiscovered, and you are no longer an adventurous man who craved discovering what worlds I hold inside me.

You slide your cup forward and smile for the first time all morning. My cue to refill you. I have been doing this for years. I'd fill your cup while you'd search the paper for the crossword puzzle for us to do. We would sit for hours and debate over the answers. We left the puzzles unfinished more often than not. Our hands would lose our pens, and end up in each others. And then suddenly who had the right answer for "7 DOWN" no longer mattered. I still fill your cup, but one day, you stopped looking for the puzzles. Neither of us said anything, it was a quiet change that we both weren't ready to face. I'm not sure why I still dote on you. Follow you around, and give you what you need. No, what you *want*. All the while ignoring everything that I need.

There is always a sickening that follows. An emptiness in the pit of my stomach. I want something more than a courteous "love", and I don't quite know how to tell you, but the 'love" we share is no longer it. I try to be your everything, in hopes I would once again be something in your mind. It has been too long since I have lived there. Every now and then I knock on the door to your heart. You slowly begin to open up, but then shut it again before letting me in completely. And I am always left wanting more. Needing more. It is a twisted game we have both become accustomed to playing.

Your eyes have grown dull and there's not much light behind them. I prayed that there were still some remnants of a flame if even only a flicker. There must be some heat still burning inside that body of yours. If you would just drop your wall and let me in, I knew I could ignite it once again. But we have become silent. It was too quiet for it to be called love. But our memories are too loud for me to ignore.

We used to dance in front of this very window. We would spend all day dreaming about what was to come that night, but would wait until the sky went black to speak of it. We could smell it on each other. It would linger as we passed in the halls and our fingertips kissed.

We would reach for each other. A silent invitation meant for a party of two. And when the sky would finally turn black, the moonlight would shine in brighter than the street light that flickered throughout the night. We would dance until our hunger grew to be too much. And even though we were all alone in the house, we tiptoed as we searched for a corner of the room where no one could find us. Not even the moon that was still peaking through the window. We would find each other in the darkness and get lost together once more. Swaying to the music, even when it wasn't playing. A rhythm that could only be heard when we were one. When our tongues went silent. When our bodies kissed.

It's been so long since we made music together and now all I hear is the drumming of your fingertips while you sip your coffee. You chuckle now and then, look up from your paper and smile at me. It's a polite smile. Too familiar and far too empty. But these days you give me so little, I take what I can. I hold on to all the small moments and pray if I mash them together hard enough, that they'll grow into something bigger.

"He hasn't forgotten how to love me. He hasn't forgotten how to love me." I repeat over and over in my mind. I'm not sure if it's true or not. It's more of a silent plea to God than anything else. A wish upon every star my eyes have danced across.

I sit silently and stare out the window. The warmth of the sun is a reminder of the warmth your skin once brought me. Your hand on my thigh, a pulse I was never able to ignore. But now, something I can barely remember.

I reach across the table and fill your cup.

"Tell me that you haven't forgotten. That you hold me somewhere in the back of your mind and still remember how things used to be. I know what we have become, but tell me that you remember. You must remember. Maybe you are happy with quiet love. An almost too gentle love. Your polite kisses on the cheek and the same "goodnight dear" haunt me. And we, my lost love, have become my greatest fear."

He puts the paper down and reaches across the table. I straighten my spine and lean into him, praying that he was finally missing the way we used to dance. Your hands reach right past mine and grab the sugar.

"I just need a little more sweetness to get me through the day." He chuckles and I know that things will never again be what they used to.

LINGERS

Yesterday still lingers.
Bittersweet on my lips.
Reminding me that you and I
are so much more
than a moment.

But you, you were never
one to pay attention to the clock.
A moment, a lifetime, a second...
they all last the same in your mind.

And you and I, are easily forgotten.

PAPER BAGS

I'm not the shot of whiskey you take to get by.
I'm not even the empty paper bag
you brought your bottle home in.
I'm a million things
but nothing that you need at this moment.
I am your everything and nothing all rolled into an ugly ball
that you are willing to throw to the dogs.
And tonight, after a million and one nights
of wishing to be so much more,
I'm still at your side.

BROKEN

Minutes. An eternity.
The daylight drifts away,
and you and I are no closer
than the night before.
Your body aches for mine.
My body screams all of the things
that are begging to be let out.
But the silence kills all.
Daylight breaks,
and we have lost all but the moment
before our promises
were broken in the dark.

LOST

I can't promise that I won't look for you
when you don't want to be found.
I hear the words,
like a clap of thunder that doesn't even
attempt to quiet itself.
It booms its way into my heart
and tramples over every truth
that I had been holding on to.
But only for a moment.

I don't hold on to these feelings.
I've learned to let go.
Because you needing to be "lost"
is too lonesome for my soul.
And I know that one day,
you'll come looking for me
and beg me to pull you back in.

AWAKE

I dreamt of you. Of the love that we make.
Not of what could be. But what has been. What is.
I dreamt of the nights we fell into each other.
Knowing that at any moment we could fall
and not be afraid of the drop.

I dreamt of us taking a leap and falling so damn hard,
but never hitting bottom.
Floating mid-air, between all of our dreams
and every single fear.
Of reaching for you, only to find you
already reaching back for me.
I dreamt of knowing we were so much more than a dream,
and not being afraid to wake up and lose it all.

I dreamt.
I dreamt.
I dreamt.

And then, I woke up.

HERE

Tonight there are words pressing
against my spine.
Forcing me to stand straight
when all I want to do is sleep.
I try to bury them inside.
Deep down to the bottom of my soul.
A place so often left alone. So often quiet.
I don't let just anyone in. I barely visit myself.

They sit. They linger.
They stir the air and choke me
as they fight their way up.
I have so much to say but nothing will come out.
I scream and only silence greets the air.
My tears fall and I am silent.
I have no right to this.
It's all unplanned. Unwanted.
But even when I close my eyes,
this truth is still here.

And you are not.

ELSEWHERE

It's no longer the moans that we
try to keep quiet in the night.
It's no longer my touch that
you reach for.
I dream of all that we used to be.
You say nothing has changed.
But I feel it.
You still crave all that I do,
you're just looking somewhere else for it.

FORGET

I think maybe we have forgotten
our beginning. The magic.
The quiet nights away from the world,
where only our whispers lived.
When there was nothing but our breath
to bounce off the stars in the sky.
No other voices to be heard.
No other lips to taste.

I think you have forgotten that I am
what you once craved more than the sunlight.
More than the moonlight sweeping into your windows.
More than the music you made before me.
We have forgotten to remember that the distance
between our bodies grows more each day.

And if we don't fight to keep this tether tied,
then one of us is bound to break free.
And this world is too dark and twisted
to find our way back.

I think we have forgotten
how easy it has become to forget.

KNOCK KNOCK

I wasn't supposed to let you in.
You weren't supposed to come knocking.
And despite every rule, we have before us,
we are both standing at the door to our love,
wondering who will open their arms first.

ROAD MAPS

You don't touch me like you used to.
Your hands seem as if they belong
to someone new.
Maybe that's my fault. Pushing you away.
So afraid you'd see past the smoke and mirrors
and feel everything I am made of.

In my mind, I am more than curves.
I am mountains. Nearly impossible to conquer.
And I have been so afraid to find out if you would really
want to travel my roads.
Without a road map, I fear you'd get lost.

MISTAKES AND OTHER THINGS WE CALL IT

I am afraid. I am afraid that I will never be exactly what you are looking for. And if I am being honest, I am afraid that I will never be who you are looking for. I will never be her. No, I won't know the words to all of your favorite songs the way she did (but I still try to learn them). My skin won't smell the way hers did (I know vanilla is your favorite scent, but I still soak myself in florals). My hair won't fall against your face the way hers did (her curls fell from her head and tickled your cheek, while my hair sits flat against my back). *I will never be her.*

You say that you don't want her. That mine is the only body you want to become one with. But you remember that night, don't you? That night told me a different story. With her hair brushing against your cheek. Her hand on your thigh, and yours, not pushing hers away. That night. That night the world changed for both of us. I wasn't even there and I remember.

Candles lit *"for better lighting"*, she told you, *"It's so hard to get good lighting in this room."*

Cigarettes and half-empty beer cans littered the nightstands. A gin bottle to your left; your favorite. So fresh, that the dust didn't have time to settle. on the bottle. She was ready for you. Your music playing, like a movie soundtrack to remember the night by. The two of you sitting on the edge of her bed.

"Far enough to remain safe," you thought.

Obviously, not far enough. At least that is how I remember it. I replay that night over and over again in my mind. Each time the story changes ever so slightly. She moves in first. No, you moved in first. Either way, the ending is always the same. You, months later, drunkenly telling me that her lips landed on yours. That somehow, your bodies ended up on the same bed. In the same room. On the same night, you told me, "Nothing is wrong. I am just tired." And I, like always, believed you.

"She needed a friend." You said over and over again., trying to convince me that your heart was in the right place. Maybe you were trying to convince yourself. Your intentions may have been clean, but you knew she was looking for more than a friend.

And somehow, she crept her way into your heart. She didn't steal it all or even steal a piece of you. She just took up enough room to push me aside for the night. But she wasn't only trying to creep into your heart, was she? No, she was too busy trying to creep into your pants. You swear to me that she never made it. That her lips landing on yours was as far as your "mistake" went.

"I messed up," you said to me.

You spoke as if you had spilled milk all over the counter and were praying that I didn't start to cry. And you don't even pray. It's funny, I looked into your eyes and I couldn't tell who you felt worse for, you or me. Maybe it was the alcohol talking that night. Let's call it liquid courage. Maybe your truth was not meant to come out.

"I just didn't know how to tell you."

Those were your words to me as your friends stood on the other side of our living room. Music blaring so high they couldn't hear my pain, but close enough to see it. Ten feet away, watching from the sidelines as I try to leave, but you pull me in close. You wanted me close that night. After months of pushing me away, while I fought to be by your side. And it wasn't until now, that you say you wanted me there. But did you want me there? Or was it that you just didn't want me far away? I don't think you knew the real truth.

The funny thing is, she danced in my mind even before that

night. From the first time that I met her and saw you two together. I could see she still carried a piece of you with her. It might not have been your heart that she still held on to, but she had a hold on you. And I've spent years worrying that I will never be her. My hair isn't that deep chestnut brown that I know you love so much. I've tried. But that shade doesn't make my eyes shine the way hers do. And believe me, I know. I've spent hours looking at pictures. Trying to see if I could match my smile to

hers. Maybe then you would be inclined to kiss me the way I am sure she kissed you that night.

But no. I am not her. And as hard as I may have prayed, because *I do pray*, I will never be her. As much as you may have wanted it, be glad. I will never be her. I will never sneak into the head of another man with the intention of finding my way into his bed. A man whose heart is already attached. A man whose hand already clings to another's during the dark hours of the night.

I am not her. Those lyrics don't spill from my tongue the way they spilled from hers. And now that I know about the music you two have made, they never will. I know that some days, she shows up in your mind, if not your heart. How could she not? You were willing to risk it all. Or maybe, at that time, there wasn't anything to risk. Maybe the weight of my love didn't even register compared to the dreams of her that you had been holding on to. I know you had been carrying them around for years. Tucked in your back pocket, praying that they would one day slip away. But then, one night, like it was fate (or that's what you told yourself), she came into town. Looking for a "friend" and yours was the first name that came to mind.

I always wonder if she knew about me. Did my name fall from her lips? From yours? I don't see how it would. Yours were busy. Your lips were too busy mimicking the dance of her own. I like to imagine that you preached of your love for me. That my name dripped from your lips and every syllable molded together and became a beautiful song. An anthem of our love. But we both know the real story,

You two had been telling tales for years. Secrets held between the palms of your hands. Never meant to be heard by anyone other than the two of you. But here I am, trying to piece together the pieces torn and thrown into the wind. Trying to figure out if there is more to your story, or if that chapter is over.

TOO MUCH

Sun-kissed moments.
We were one. Drenched in our love.
A moment alone; together.
It seems it would take a lifetime to forget.
You gave in to me. I never had to ask.

You reached, I let you.
You grabbed, I released.
You promised, I believed.

And that is the moment our story began.
I wanted more.
You gave an inch, and then some.
You took my body, but only after I gave it all to you.
I never asked for it back, just for one more touch.

How quickly that became too much for you.

HOLLOW AND HOLES

It is almost as if the words never leave my lips.
I hear them echoing down the hall,
vibrating within every hollow and hole
where our memories once hung.
They have left me. I have sent them your way.
But you refuse to take them in.
You won't claim them.
You won't even hold them in the palm of your hand
and wish them to be something else.
Because if you laid one finger on them,
gave one breath to them,
looked at them in an almost believing way,
you might see the truth that lies inside these words.
And we both know,
you'd never be able to look away.

THE LAST TIME

You walked into the room
and I remembered what it felt like
to crave your body.

It used to cover me like a blanket.
Keeping me from feeling the chill
sent my way on a cold winter day.
You would wrap your arms around me
and tease me with a warmth I so desperately needed.

I breathe you in, trying to remember the last time
I craved more than a memory.
Now, we are nothing more than that.
A distant memory that we are both afraid to wake.

SCRIBBLES

I found your letter.
Little hearts scribbled in the corner.
"I love you" at the top of the page.
"Forever yours" at the bottom.
A pledge to your love and signed by your name.
1,000,001 promises of your love.
Everything I had waited
so long to hear.
The page was littered with letters,
but none of them spelled out my name.

DRUNKEN DREAMS

"Look at me," you begged me. "I promise it will be ok. We will be ok."

You whispered this over and over again. Hoping that if you said it enough times, I would finally believe you. We had been sitting at that table for an hour. Maybe three. I wasn't quite sure how long we have been playing these same lines on repeat. Our words were beginning to bleed together and my "no" was starting to sounds like an "ok".

You reminded me of your love. Begged me to listen. And I, I have grown so tired of trying to tie my ears shut. I gave in. Opened my ears, but not my heart. That, I was still holding on to. But for now, you have my attention. You spewed your stories. Your tales of broken promises that we should forget. Practically made a list of every mistake against my soul. Laid out on the table. So neat, tidy. Like freshly cleaned laundry, but so ready to break my heart all over again.

I lost myself in that list and forgot to listen to all of the "good" that you were promising. You called my name. Not once, but three times before I snapped out of it. I gave up on feeling the pain and listened once more. You tried to replace the list of pain with promises of all of the happiness that was to come our way. All of the smiles that would soon wipe away any memory of tears that once lived within me.

But I didn't believe you. I don't know how to believe you anymore. We tell the same stories to each other. Over and over again. We've been trying to dance in this rainstorm for years. Passing tissues off as memories that we want to hold on to and treasure, instead of tossing aside to forget about. We write stories down in our hearts and make-believe that someday the lines will blur together and make sense.

But the rain fogs our mirrors and we can't see our reflection anymore. Is this our sober reality? Or a drunken dream? Lately, I can't seem to tell the difference. So for now, all I can say is, "I know."

EMPTY SKIES

I was made for you.
Or at least that is what I thought.
Every fiber of my being
was etched in the sky for you.
Written out in stars.
To be held in your hands, but never captured.
To be loved, but not controlled.
To be missed, but never forgotten.

But today I find myself trying to
sneak back into your heart.
The sky in your eyes has gone black
and I can no longer see our story
written in them.

ROADS

It's a burning sensation.
A fire deep inside me.
Not one of passion and heat,
but the end of something.
I want to call for you.
Make you hear my voice.
But your ears have been shut
to the only tune my mouth can sing.
You no longer listen for the melody
that I have created just for you.
And once again, we are separated
by more than just miles.
And tonight I know,
I am the only one willing
to travel the dark roads.

ENDINGS

I can feel it coming. Our ending.
It taunts me while I try to sleep
and dream only of our love.
Is it the end of us?
I don't know.
But I feel as though
the winds are changing.
You're being pulled in one direction,
and I, in the other.
We can't seem to find our way
back to each other.
And I can't help but feel
that you have already stopped looking.

JUST A MOMENT

I want to call out to you.
Pick up the phone and make you hear
everything that is building up inside me.
I want you to hear it in my voice.
Feel everything that I feel.
I need you to say everything
that I have been waiting to hear.
I pray and I pray and I pray...
"Say it all."

But would it all be a lie?
You, reading from a page of my heart,
rather than your own,
would that do anything other than soothe my soul
for a lonely moment or two?

SINK OR SWIM

It's all too familiar.
This echo in your voice.
There is too much air.
Too much distance.
Too much of our past.
You say that times have changed.
That we are more than where
we came from.
But how do you not sink beneath
the weight of it all?
Does our story not pull you under?
It floods my mind as I try to sleep.
I fight to swim to the shore,
but I can't help but take it all on.
I am drowning in everything that we were,
and fighting so hard to reach everything
you say we are.

EVERYTHING

What if tomorrow doesn't take me anywhere?
And I am still stuck here dreaming of everything that
we were meant to be?

NUMB

If I called your name, would you hear me?
Would you listen to each letter
as it dripped from my lips?
Savor every moment that I spent letting
you live within my heart?

Or would you turn away?
Have I called for you too many times?
Reached for you too often?
Are your arms are tired of reaching back?
Or are you simply numb to the sound of your name
escaping my mouth?

THIS LOVE

I wish I could feel the way you do.
Take us past all of the emptiness
that hangs around like it's here to stay.
It stands on empty street corners;
parks in empty lots, just to sit and wait.
It peaks its head in;
just enough to remind us that it is still here.
Waiting and waiting.

We have been fighting wars with open arms.
Almost welcoming any distraction from our truth.
I wish we could hunt down the devil
that dances inside our minds.
He is heartless, cruel.
And I know, he has no cares for
the hours, years, lifetimes we've put into this love.

And I am worried, that neither do you.

THIRSTY

I am empty.
Beyond empty, I am thirsty.
Longing for the warmth that used
to rush over me,
I can no longer feel you.
Like a river with nowhere to bend,
or an ocean without sand to crash upon.
I am longing for something so familiar
but so far away.
How do I find it all once again?
How do I find something
that doesn't want to be found?

BURNT COFFEE

I can still taste you on my tongue.
Bitter, like burnt coffee.
You used to be my addiction, my high.
I would swallow you up,
and let you seep into my body.
Rushing through my veins
and bringing me back to life.
Just a momentary high;
you were my double shot.
And I would swallow you whole.
In one gulp.
Never knowing that it might be my last
taste of you.

SILENCE

I am searching for answers on these empty roads.
The street lights all claim to have a different song.
But every time I stop to listen,
I hear the same damn tune.
All of their lyrics echo in my mind.
There is no real escape.

I keep driving.
I'm on a mission to find something
that I am not even sure exists anymore.
I carry road maps that swore they would
lead me into the arms of a real lover.
But I still can't seem to find my way.
I am lost on the back roads.
Twisting and winding; with no end in sight.
And left forever driving with my radio down
and an empty passenger seat.

TOUCHED

I have touched you in a thousand different ways.
Through the palm of my hand
on the small of your back.
When our shoulders kissed as we slept.
I have felt your fingers dance across my face
as you push the hair from my eyes.

But somehow, you now feel foreign.
Your skin is colder than I remember and
my fingers can't seem to find their way
between yours.

You haven't pulled away,
but you have stopped reaching.
That is an almost scarier truth.
There is no wanting in your voice.
No silently calling my name in the dark.

There is just silence and I am left
missing so much more than you touching me
in the dark.

RUN

We say the same words over and over again.
They have lost all meaning.
All power.
I don't even try to hear them.
The harder I try to listen,
the more I want to run.
Run away from you for saying the
same damn thing again.
Run away because I have been
standing still for far too long.
Run away because right now,
anywhere else has to be less painful than this.

STORIES

You say that you're telling me the truth.
I laugh. How can you tell me the truth
when you don't even really know it?
You carry stories with you.
Some are born out of our truth,
others are versions you tell yourself
to help you sleep at night.
Do you even know the difference anymore?
Are you reaching from different books?
Or have you molded all stories into one?
I wanted to be more than a story to be told,
I wanted to be a tune you can't get out of your head.

AFTERMATH

Have you ever awoken from the pain
of heartbreak?
Felt like you were drowning,
but suddenly could swim?
Tasted a drink of water
after what felt like a hundred years of thirst?

That's what it felt like to be over you.

BED TIME STORIES

I miss our talks.
The way your lips used to chase after my name
like a drop of water in a sun scorched desert.
After hours of not knowing which way to turn,
and suddenly finding a map.

I miss your grip.
The way you would hold my words in the palm
of your hand and still let me finish my sentence.
As if you were the page, and I, the sonnet
that was about to be written.

I miss your footsteps.
The way they echoed behind mine.
Far enough to let me breathe.
But close enough to catch up.

I miss it all.
I miss you.

NEVER AGAIN

Do you remember the day that you knew that our love was starting to die? I remember the day I knew it was over. You were there. Well, you were at my side. Your body might have been with me, but your mind was with her. Daydreaming of nights I didn't yet know about. Moments that we should have shared, but were spent on her.

We laid in our bed. Bodies stretched out, but not even close to touching. I wanted to reach for you. I miss the days of your head resting on my stomach. You would listen for my breaths and try to slow yours to match my pace. It had been so long since our bodies were in sync. Maybe deep down I knew the ending was coming, but my heart wasn't ready to admit it. My body wasn't ready to not touch you again.

I couldn't resist any longer, and I blindly reached out for you. My hand landed on your thigh, begging to send shock waves through you. You kept your eyes closed and didn't move. I thought maybe you fell asleep. But now I wonder, were you wishing me away? Or simply wishing I was her? I am not sure which one would be better. I let my hand sit for a moment, and then began to trace the seem of your jeans up your thigh. You shifted. Not enough to say you were playing along, just enough to make things uncomfortable. I pulled away and sat up.

"Where are you?" I asked.

You let out a big sigh, and threw your hands over your face.

"I'm not in the mood for games. What do you want?" You rolled on your side and pulled out your phone. The volume was up so high, it was obvious you had no intention of listening for my response.

"I just miss you. We haven't touched in so long, it feels like you're miles away. And I don't know how to reach you anymore, or if you even want me to."

"I'm too tired for this. We're fine." You huffed as you walked away. You didn't look back. You already knew what was waiting; quiet tears running down my ivory cheeks. You're no stranger to the path they travel from my eyes. You know they are there, you just no longer care enough to wipe them away.

I didn't move. I sat in the same bed that we had made love in so many times before. Spent nights laughing and watching old scary movies. Well, we would start to watch movies, and ended up lost in each other's arms.

I closed my eyes and tried to remember the last time this bed felt any love and I couldn't. And I could tell by the tone of your voice, it probably never would again.

ABSENCE

I wonder if you think of me.
Does your mind travel my way
when our bodies are separated
by more than miles?
Do you feel the weight of empty sheets?
Draped across your naked chest,
the way my hair used to fall across you.
You are at my side, and I still feel your absence.
There is an emptiness that stays,
even when you return.

CREEP

You compared me to the moonlight.
Waited all day for me to arrive,
and once I was in your sight,
you closed your eyes
and started dreaming of something else.

I gave you everything you ever asked for,
and still, when the quiet hours of the night crept in,
I wasn't enough.

MINE

"You are mine."
Three words. That is all I craved.
All I wanted to hear.
But somehow, those words
were too heavy for you to carry.
Too loud for you to speak.
So, you buried them deep in your pockets.
Hoping they would find themselves forgotten.

But I, I would cross my heart and swear
in front of judge and jury,
that you were all I needed.
Everything I wanted to love.
And even more, everything I thought I needed.
Until I didn't.

FORGIVE

This love is not enough.
It aches, and screams.
It asks nothing of me,
except an apology for being gone.

But I am not ready to forgive.

AGAIN

I know I will see you again.
Some day, down the road.
When we both have had enough time
to watch every wrong decision fade away.
When we forget the "no's"
that should have been a "yes".
And give up trying to hold on to every last breath
that left us as we spoke each other's names.

To step back from all that stood in our way.
Forget the nights we slept without
each other's arms wrapped around us.
And took our chances fighting with the rain.
Arguing who could carry more tears.

I know I will see you again.
I can't get you off my mind.
And even though you never call,
I hear it when we speak.
Your silence says so much more
than your mouth ever will.

LANES

We're shifting lanes and veering off course.
Memories from a lifetime ago;
they never really go away.
They haunt me for a moment and then,
I am reminded of how we found our way back.
Back to one another without a map.
We stayed our course, side by side.
Walking down the road together.
Quietly searching for answers to the questions
that we were both too afraid to ask.
And now we are drowning in a sea of doubt.
Our voices have been lost in the wind.
And you and I are so far
from where we should be.

SHADOWS

We walked together.
Side by side,
avoiding shadows and dark corners.
We knew our weaknesses.
Our love only grew in the dark.
So we stayed in the sunlight.
Praying we would be able
to avoid dark alleys and the
possibility of love creeping back up.
But, as always, the sun eventually goes down,
and it's time for us to go our separate ways.
We were meant for just a moment
of passion, nothing more.
A love like ours creeps in and strangles
the life out of both of us.

So, we will be left forever dancing in the sunlight,
avoiding the shadows at all costs.

FAULT

I'm beginning to see the fault
that sleeps in your eyes.
It only comes out at night.
When the shadows you so easily
lurk behind, disappear and, you,
you are left with nothing
but your nakedness to bathe in.

ACCIDENTS

We fall asleep beneath the sheets.
Our hands barely touch.
And if they do, it's by accident.
You're content with living on one side of the bed.
Quiet. Angry.
So purposely distanced yourself from me.
From my body. From my being.
I waited for you to walk through the doors.
My eyes were shut the entire time.
But we both knew I wasn't sleeping.
I wanted to say your name.
And you, you wanted nothing more
then to be somewhere else.

SLIPPING

You are a foolish man.
You say that you are waiting
for a sign from the Gods;
they will tell you which way to run.
Into my arms or back out to sea.
But I don't even believe in the tales you tell.
Your stories have lived in my heart
for too long and I've lost too much
of myself in the waiting.

You can watch the skies
for a sign from above.
But I promise you,
you will miss how quickly
I start to slip away.

LOVE YOU

Emptiness filled the room. We laid, as we had laid, a million nights before. Backs against each other. You faced the door... an escape you'd been dreaming about for years. And I, my face to the wall. A blank slate. I wanted to lose myself in what seemed like a deep sea of nothingness. A blinding abbess. I thought if I stared long and still enough, I would be able to find all of our answers. Our truths. But all I found were the memories we have tried so hard to forget.

We are silent. Heat rising from our bodies. Nowhere to go, except back inside us once again. In and out we breathe. Our breath bouncing off the ceiling and beating down on our chest. Each thump is a reminder of how much we wished we were back in each other's arms. But we are nowhere near that. We are stuck inside this moment; with nothing but tears and empty sighs to kiss us goodnight.

I rolled over and pulled my pillow to my chest. I don't remember the last time you pulled me in this close. Close enough to smell the day-old perfume dancing on my neck. Close enough to feel my body rise and fall as I take a breath and breathe you in. But now there is a wall between us. Built by the months of silence we have been living with. Neither of us fighting to make any noise between our bodies, let alone any music.

You rolled over first; missing my entrance by seconds. Almost intentional. You barely waited for me to walk out of the bathroom. That used to be too much for you to handle. Me, walking out of the bathroom. A cloud of steam following as my hair was still dripping from the shower. But now you roll over to avoid contact. Are you afraid to touch me? Have you forgotten how to do it? Or are you no longer interested?

Our late night cuddles and sweet whispers of nothing have been replaced with an empty:

"Night. Love you."

There is no "I" in your proclamation of love. You take no claim in it. Your voice gets quieter and quieter each night. And It is almost as if you don't want the words to belong to you.

EXHALE

What did I come here for?
I've been so tired of being gone.
Knowing all that I am missing,
and trying so hard to forget that you miss nothing.
Not the small of my back that your hand knows so well.
Not the way my body moves in the darkness.
Closer and closer to you, for nothing more than your
breath on my neck.
You miss nothing of the way your body arches
as I move in closer.
Making space in a world that seemed far too full.

It wasn't too long before I realized that
you welcomed my absence.
You got high on my scent lingering a little less each day.
And just when it was almost gone,
you call me back, but just for a moment.
Long enough to convince me to stay,
knowing you wanted nothing more
than a exhale or two.

CRAVINGS

You told me not to fall.
That loving you would sting more
than a shot of whiskey.
You would burn me from the inside out,
and I would never see it coming.
That there would be no chaser
to wash your taste away.

But I craved you.
My heart was thirsty for something
so much more than comfort.
And you, you were my escape.
A high I knew I didn't need,
and that made me want you so much more.
I didn't need you. I wanted you.

You warned me; soon you'd be gone.
And like an addiction I couldn't beat,
I'd be left wanting so much more.

AIR

You are distant. Cold.
You say that you are here, but you are not.
Your eyes avoid mine like a flame avoids the rain.
You inch further away as I move in closer.
I can feel it in the air,
there are a million different places
that you would rather be.

5 DAYS

It's been 5 days. I walked away and I haven't looked back. I had been planning it for so long. All the words I would say. All the tears I would hold back. I planned my every step. Every movement. Every breath. How close I would stand to you. Close enough for you to reach out, but far enough so you couldn't touch me. My arms crossed like a solider ready for war. We both knew we were going to battle. I wanted so badly to leave and I knew you'd fight for me to stay. But not because you wanted me here. You just didn't want me anywhere else. And that wasn't enough for me anymore.

And here I am. Gone. We went to battle that night. The words flew from our lips like bullets. Faster than either of us saw coming. We didn't want to kill each other, but we knew that wounding our love would be the same thing. And even though we had far more hits than misses, we both walked our separate ways with battle scars we knew would never fade away.

I finally made my escape. I was no longer trapped in your web or losing myself in your arms. I thought I would be throwing confetti and dancing under the moon. Blaring every song you hate; full volume. Over and over. Secretly wishing that you'd somehow hear it. I thought I would be leaving towels on the floor and my hair swirled on the shower wall (all of the things you hate the most). But I haven't seen the shower walls in 6 days. Not since the last time I was in your arms. The night before we went to battle. We both had known the war was coming, but needed one more night of peace. We laid together. Side by side. Breathing in as hard as we could. Trying to soak up every last bit of the love that was in the air.

I can still smell you on me. I'm still wearing that same shirt. Your shirt. You slipped it on me the night before. Now it's covered in dry, salty tears and mascara. Proof that you wounded me more than I wanted to admit. I can't take it off. I should be dancing. Damn it. I should be dancing so hard. But I can't move. Your side of the bed is so empty and I am frozen by the fear that it will never be filled again.

TUCK & HIDE

There is no point in hiding the truth.
Everything we try to tuck under
our pillow at night.
Every bump and hurdle
that we have tried to put to sleep.
Every deep sigh that we
were trying to hide.

The night is over, and the sun
is shining, bright.
Our secrets have nowhere to hide.
And the truth is, I think we have stopped looking
The only hope for this us
is to find love somewhere else.

RETURN TO SENDER

You won't give me your all.
You give me little more than
your pieces of nothing.
Not even enough pieces worth gluing together.
That ugly mess you left on my doorstep.
Like a package that you shipped to me
without a return address,
you thought I would just accept it.
No questions asked,
But here I am, trying to peel back your layers
and open you up.
I just want to discover what's inside.
I don't want the pieces you
wish to discard.
I want the pieces you are holding on to.
The ones worth more than
their weight in gold.
I am not looking to cash them in,
I just want to see all that you once wanted to,
but are no longer willing to share with me.

IGNORE

I know that I am not supposed to care.
My heart tells me this every day.
But the thought of your fingers
dancing across her skin,
to the same tune that they used
to dance on mine...
well, that is hurt that I can't ignore.

ENOUGH

Did you know that you were enough?
At that moment. Quiet and quick,
when our bodies bled together and for a second,
I couldn't tell us apart.
You were enough.
But once the music faded and
our bodies drifted apart,
you were like a stranger.
And I finally realized that I needed
so much more.

KNOWN

I wish I could say that you knew me
in the ways that I wanted to be known.
That in a crowded room, you would
hear a sigh and know it belonged to me.
That you would catch it in the palm of your hand,
keep it warm and hold onto it until
you returned it to me.

I wish you knew that when my heart
begins to beat faster, it means that
I need you to move closer not try to slip away.
To pull me into you and fall asleep
before you remember to let go.

I wish you knew that my "Goodbye, I'm done"
was laced with so much wanting. That part of me
wanted you to reach out to me one more time.
so I could see that I wasn't the only one fighting for us.
But at the same time, I wanted myself to walk away
and never look back.

BENT

Our love was twisted and turned in ways
that I am not sure a love should go.
It bent at the slightest ache and curved
when the winds weren't blowing our way.

We were not a straight line.
Nothing was black or white between us.
We were a sandstorm in a bottle
and our love way slowly beginning to drown.

ENTRAPMENT

And still, I find myself missing your hand
wrapped around my own.
Were you a pocket to hold me inside?
Or a lock to hold me hostage?
Either way, I miss being entrapped
by all that you are.

ENDINGS

This ending wasn't our fault.
It wasn't in the plans we had laid out
that night beneath the dark sky.
When we swore that our love was written in the stars.
Only to wake one night and find that the stars
had begun to fade away,
and our sky had turned completely black.
You turned to me, eyes locked on mine,
and begged me not to look away.

*"We've found each other. Out of all the emptiness
this world wanted us to lose ourselves in,
we found each other. Promise me that if we start to fade,
you will look for me. Because, even if the sky is completely dark, I will never stop looking for you."*

And now I lay beneath a star-littered sky.
An empty spot on the sheet next to me,
as if the stars still spell out "forever" for you.
I stopped praying that you were still looking for me.
Days turned into months, and before I knew it,
I couldn't remember the last time we sat together.

ESCAPE

We have been trying to escape this for years.
This ending. This goodbye.
We've tried to fight our way through the fog.
Running together into the sea,
we would try to jump the tide.
And with our arms still locked,
we fought to swim to shore.

But the waves always managed
to pull us under.
They forced us to see all we so
desperately try to forget.
Our tether that we once tied together
was not a chain, dragging us down.
It was no longer sink or swim,
we knew the only way out of this alive
would be our goodbye.

SONGS TO LIVE BY

Maybe it's the right song,
at the wrong time,
making me wish you were still here.
I hear it in my head; it plays only for me.
Bouncing off the back of my closed eyes,
it's keeping me awake at night.
Creeping in my mind
and retelling me all of the stories
that I have been trying to forget.
You left, and the music kept playing;
almost to the beat
of your footsteps walking away.
Our song to live by
became your song to leave by.

MAGIC

Take me back to the time
when your arms were wrapped
around my naked frame.
Your skin on my skin.
Your breath on my breath.
More than ecstasy,
we were magic.

And then, poof, you were gone.

QUIET

Maybe it wasn't heaven that we lost ourselves in.
The stars didn't align for us.
And despite all the rain that fell from the sky,
putting out our flames,
the thunder stopped clapping for us.
The heavens went quiet, and it was in that moment
that I knew our days were numbered.

DWELLINGS

Does this emptiness only dwell within me?
Do you feel the silence that we have
begun to drown in?
Or do you tune it out?
It crashes upon me,
like a wave trying to escape the sea.
Pulling me under and stealing my breath
without a promise of returning it.

BEFORE & AFTER

Confusion fills the air,
and it tastes like so many nights
before this one.

THE LAST TIME

You walked into the room
and I remembered what it felt like
to crave your body.

It used to cover me like a blanket.
Keeping me from feeling the chill
sent my way on a cold winter day.
You would wrap your arms around me,
and tease me with a warmth I so desperately needed.

I breathe you in, trying to remember the last time
I craved more than a memory.
Now, we are nothing more than that.
A distant memory that we are both afraid to wake.

WEAK

I don't want to seem weak.
So I keep my mouth shut and
my hands on the wheel.
I want to speak.
Make you speak.
Make you reach for me.
I want you to inch closer and
grab my thigh.
Even if its forced,
I want you to make yourself
feel our love.
But you don't care enough to
do any of this on your own.
I could do it.
Move closer and reach out to you.
I could call your name,
praying the sound of my voice pulls you in.
I could do so many things.
But I don't want to seem weak.

NOISE

When the world goes silent,
my heart begins to scream.
And despite all the noise,
no one comes to save me.

SAND

Eventually, the sun went down.
And just as I had feared,
my love has fallen asleep.
You no longer wake me when
the sun kisses your cheek.
You don't touch me
when the wind begins to warm
and your soul needs to be cooled down.

You have melted away.
Become one with the sea,
and just like every grain of sand
that I have ever held,
I fear I will never touch you again.

HURRICANE

We were not a straight line.
Nothing black and white between us.
Every day was a hurricane.
Winds raging. Rain falling.
We were a sandstorm in a bottle.
And the only thing more dangerous
then this storm, was our love.

FRONT PORCH

I waited for you.
I prayed, that like a storm,
you would come rolling in.
I was front porch sitting, watching the
lightening dance across the sky.
Wind in the trees, mixed with an echo
of your voice...
"goodbye".

Fingertips tapping on my window
are replaced with the rain drops
taunting me with your absence.
You calling out to me stays within my soul.
It shakes my walls like thunder and reminds me
that I am weathering this storm alone.

TOGETHER

Together never felt so close and so far away
at the same time.

ABOUT THE AUTHOR

My name is Jessie Michelle and in this crazy life, I wear many different titles. I am a woman and a poet. I am a partner, a mother and a daughter. A sister and a friend. But most of all, I am a lover. I am a self proclaimed addict of love and coffee. And I firmly believe that a little of each (mainly love) will solve and heal most things. I write about many facets in life, including love, heartbreak and body positivity. I was born in Virginia and spent my early childhood living in Hawaii and in Florida. I currently live in a small(ish) town in Georgia with my husband and our three children.

I have published four books: "Conversations with the Moonlight", "Honeysuckle and Forgiveness", "Second Midnight" and now, "Cold Weather Dreams". I am currently working on my fifth book of self-love poetry. All of these works are focused on love in one way or another. Many pieces touch on the sweetness that can be found in a real love, and just as many touch on the heartache that all too often follows.

Romantic love has always held a very special place in my heart, I am a self proclaimed sap and always will be. "Conversations with the Moonlight", "Second Midnight", and "Cold Weather Dreams" are dedicated to all of the feelings that come with a romantic love.

After the birth of my third child, I felt the need/urge to write about my struggles with loving the body I know owned. "Honeysuckle and Forgiveness" is my love letter to myself. Each piece is a reminder that I should love myself even when I feel I am not deserving.

I am currently working on my 5th book of poetry , which will be a followup to "Honeysuckle and Forgiveness".

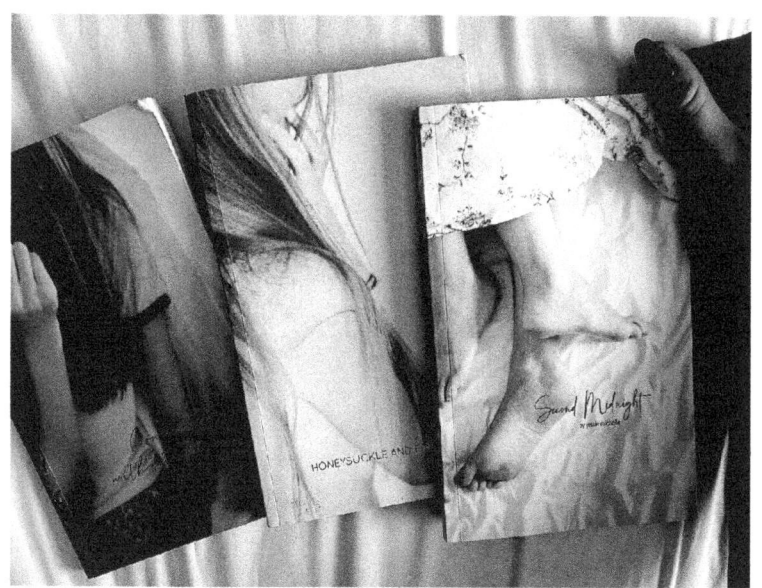

OTHER BOOKS BY JESSIE MICHELLE

"*Conversations with the Moonlight*" is a collection of words that carry the reader from the deepest levels of heartache and confusion, to the beauty of finding true love, not just in someone else, but in yourself.

"*Honeysuckle and Forgiveness*" is a step away from the usual pieces by Jessie Michelle. It is a poetry collection that helps the reader to (re)learn to love themselves. This book touches on body image, self love and acceptance.

""*Second Midnight*" is a story of long distance love. It takes the reader on a journey through all of the emotions that come to life between the moments of being in your loves arms, and the moment they leave.

All of my books are available worldwide. Find me on:

Amazon
Barnes and Noble online
The Book Depository   (worldwide distribution)
By Jessie Michelle ETSY

Made in United States
Orlando, FL
19 March 2023